Flower by Flower

Flower **by** Flower

A Practical and Inspirational Guide to the Art of Flower Arranging

by Tadhg Ryan

with Anna Selby

COURAGE
BOOKS

AN IMPRINT OF RUNNING PRESS
PHILADELPHIA • LONDON

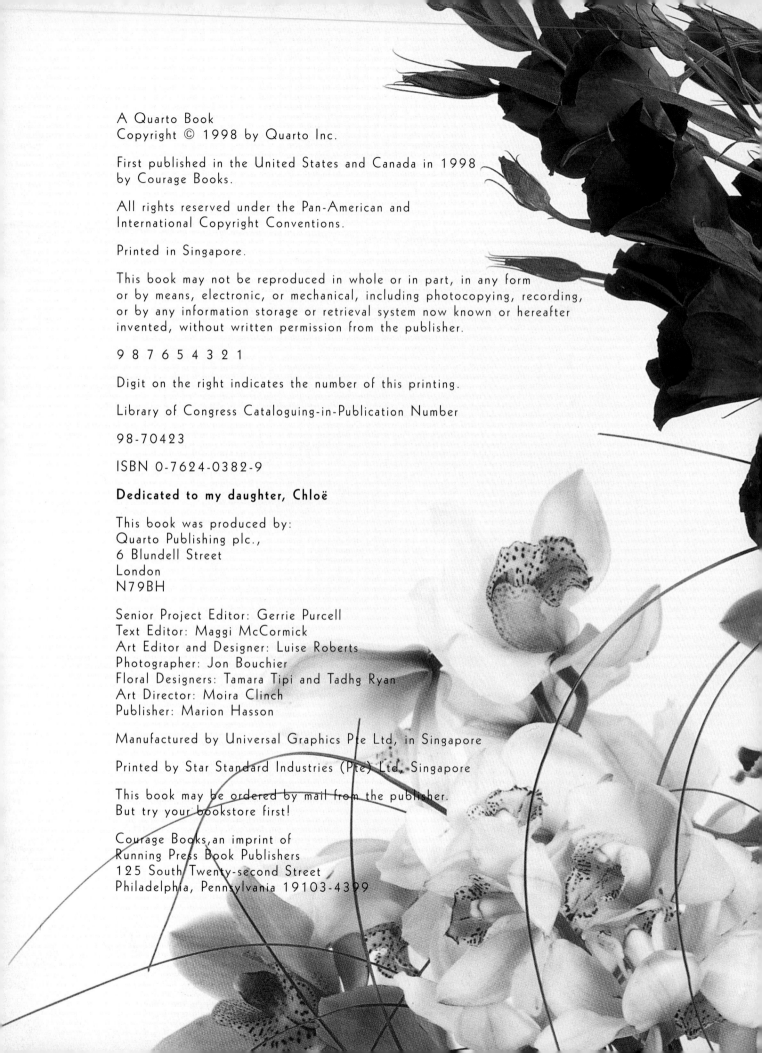

A Quarto Book
Copyright © 1998 by Quarto Inc.

First published in the United States and Canada in 1998
by Courage Books.

Printed in Singapore.

9 8 7 6 5 4 3 2 1

Digit on the right indicates the number of this printing.

Library of Congress Cataloguing-in-Publication Number

98-70423

ISBN 0-7624-0382-9

Dedicated to my daughter, Chloë

This book was produced by:
Quarto Publishing plc.,
6 Blundell Street
London
N79BH

Senior Project Editor: Gerrie Purcell
Text Editor: Maggi McCormick
Art Editor and Designer: Luise Roberts
Photographer: Jon Bouchier
Floral Designers: Tamara Tipi and Tadhg Ryan
Art Director: Moira Clinch
Publisher: Marion Hasson

Manufactured by Universal Graphics Pte Ltd, in Singapore

Printed by Star Standard Industries (Pte) Ltd, Singapore

This book may be ordered by mail from the publisher.
But try your bookstore first!

Courage Books, an imprint of
Running Press Book Publishers
125 South Twenty-second Street
Philadelphia, Pennsylvania 19103-4399

Contents

TECHNIQUES & MATERIALS
106–125

Introduction

Flowers and flower arranging are a very personal thing, and it's important to develop your own style in arrangements. This book should act as an inspiration and give you lots of ideas – but that's only the start of the learning process. Keep your eyes wide open. Inspiration, particularly in nature and the turn of the seasons, is all around you, and you will find that the more you work with flowers, the better your instinct for them becomes. Most of all, flowers are there to be enjoyed – so have fun with your arrangements!

Here, these examples are intended to help you use this book easily. The *Techniques & Materials* section gives you useful tips on caring for flowers and how to prepare them for arranging. It also includes helpful charts, on pages 114–117 and 126, with more information on many of the wonderful flowers included in this book.

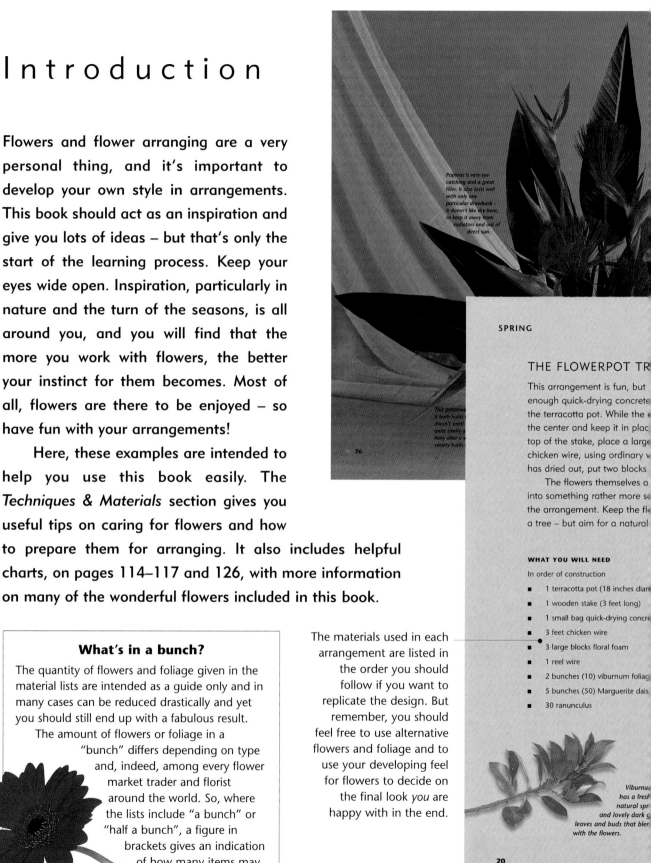

Papyrus is very eye-catching and a great filler. It also lasts well with only one particular drawback – it doesn't like dry heat, so keep it away from radiators and out of direct sun.

This preserved ... it both holds ... doesn't smell ... quite smelly a ... flaky after a ... variety holds ...

76

SPRING

THE FLOWERPOT TR

This arrangement is fun, but enough quick-drying concrete the terracotta pot. While the the center and keep it in plac top of the stake, place a large chicken wire, using ordinary v has dried out, put two blocks

The flowers themselves a into something rather more s the arrangement. Keep the fl a tree – but aim for a natural

WHAT YOU WILL NEED

In order of construction

- 1 terracotta pot (18 inches diam
- 1 wooden stake (3 feet long)
- 1 small bag quick-drying concre
- 3 feet chicken wire
- 3 large blocks floral foam
- 1 reel wire
- 2 bunches (10) viburnum foliag
- 5 bunches (50) Marguerite dais
- 30 ranunculus

Viburnu... has a fresh natural spr and lovely dark g leaves and buds that bler with the flowers.

20

What's in a bunch?

The quantity of flowers and foliage given in the material lists are intended as a guide only and in many cases can be reduced drastically and yet you should still end up with a fabulous result. The amount of flowers or foliage in a "bunch" differs depending on type and, indeed, among every flower market trader and florist around the world. So, where the lists include "a bunch" or "half a bunch", a figure in brackets gives an indication of how many items may be suitable.

The materials used in each arrangement are listed in the order you should follow if you want to replicate the design. But remember, you should feel free to use alternative flowers and foliage and to use your developing feel for flowers to decide on the final look *you* are happy with in the end.

CAGED BIRDS FLY

The strelitzia is also known as bird of paradise and comes from the Canary Islands. It is a curious mixture of the exotic and the simple. In this arrangement, the leaves are used, too, to great sculptural effect, and the overall feel is that of birds about to take flight. The strelitzia used here has wonderfully long leaves and stems – in fact these came from Italy which, at this time of year, produces the best version of this plant, as opposed to those from The Netherlands which are much shorter.

Papyrus is a great filler and very eye-catching in any arrangement, providing another sculptural element. The orange and green contrast makes this an even more striking piece, ideal for a tall table or stand. The angular positioning of both flowers and leaves is held tightly in floral foam, which is itself hidden beneath the lime-green moss.

WHAT YOU WILL NEED

In order of construction

- 1 small bird cage (9 inches high x 4 inches wide)
- ½ block floral foam

Main text gives you a background to the inspiration for the design and, in many cases, gives you examples of how you may want to use a similar arrangement.

Helpful captions give information about featured flowers and foliage – and may also suggest alternatives you could use.

of preparation. Mix up
es, or half the depth, of
ll liquid place the stake in
ncrete has dried. At the
al foam covered with
n. Once the concrete base
op of it.
e – they have been turned
nd unusual by the style of
emphasize the shape of
tight topiary feel.

Ranunculus is an old-fashioned English flower with layers of petals that radually open up. It's one of vorites.

arguerite daisies were very pular in the first years of the)s and became rather erused. They're coming ck into their own now, d are not that expensive. ey are great fun and also ke beautiful standard piary plants.

21

SPRING

spring

Spring is perhaps the most inspiring time of the year – full of anticipation and expectation – the time you can watch the trees coming gradually into bud and taking on their true shape. It is also the time of one of my absolute favorite flowers, the guelder rose (European cranberrybush), that subtle member of the viburnum family that can bring depth and interest to just about any arrangement. In fact, though, most spring flowers have a particularly wonderful quality. They have great clarity of color and are often scented, and their very freshness is a joy. You can give yourself a free rein when arranging spring flowers. There seem to be no rules about color – all seem to blend together, even the ones that shouldn't!

From the moment spring starts to arrive, new flowers seem to appear on a weekly – even a daily – basis. There are the early delicate snowdrops, golden daffodils, voluptuous tulips, as well as all the wonderful flowering branches of ornamental trees. You can, in fact, get most flowers all year round nowadays – tulips, for instance, are available twelve months a year. However, the spring itself is when spring flowers are in their prime – and at their best value. You will also find that, if you use flowers as they are in season, your arrangements will have an otherwise unobtainable freshness, as well as discovering the excitement of seeing old favorites again.

SPRING FLOWER BASKET

This is a very exuberant, colorful spring display in a rather unusual container. I've used a wire basket with an outer lining of moss which makes the flowers look as if they're growing in the most natural way. In fact, the moss is hiding an inner plastic liner which is, of course, needed so that the water doesn't seep through. Inside the liner is floral foam, and I've lined the rim with salal leaves to give the arrangement a sense of line and structure. The earthy nature of the container, together with the semi-wild anemones and thistles, gives this arrangement a simple, natural look. If you dampen the moss, you could place flowers around the base to add another dimension.

Other good combinations would be red tulips with yellow daffodils, narcissi, or primroses; or put blue anemones with white tulips or ranunculus.

WHAT YOU WILL NEED

In order of construction

- 1 wire basket (12 inches diameter)
- Floral foam
- 2 handfuls of spaghnum moss
- 1 bunch (5) salal leaves
- 9 eryngiums
- 12 'Grand Gala' red roses
- 20 anemones
- 10 ligustrum stems

Eryngiums are thistles and have a lovely electric blue color. I've used small ones here, but they do come on bigger stems, in which case one stem will actually go a long way and look stunning as part of a larger arrangement in a big vase.

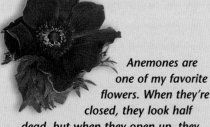

Anemones are one of my favorite flowers. When they're closed, they look half dead, but when they open up, they have true simplicity and beauty – a flower, I think, for connoisseurs.

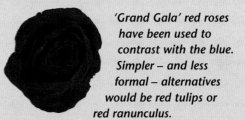

'Grand Gala' red roses have been used to contrast with the blue. Simpler – and less formal – alternatives would be red tulips or red ranunculus.

Ligustrum has beautiful black
berries, which are quite
hardy and so do not
bruise easily.

Salal leaves act as
long-lasting foliage
with good sized leaf.

FLOWERPOT GARDEN

This is the perfect beginner's arrangement – if you feel at all nervous, start here! It is actually impossible to go wrong with this arrangement – if it feels right to you, then it is right. The flowers are arranged in a shape that looks as natural as possible, as if the flowers are still alive and growing. This is certainly part of the trend of modern floristry. We have progressed from stiff, formal arrangements to those that have a much looser, easier feel.

Here, I've taken a simple terracotta pot, lined it, and filled it with floral foam. You then put the flowers in as they look right to you. With the cattails this arrangement stands around three feet tall so it makes a cheerful display centerpiece for a buffet table. If you wanted more color, you could always spray the flowerpot.

WHAT YOU WILL NEED

In order of construction

- 1 terracotta flowerpot
  (18 inches diameter)
- Floral foam
- 1 bunch bear grass (30 strands)
- 9 cattails
- 9 French tulips
- 30 irises
- 30 narcissi

French tulips are taller than other varieties and work beautifully alone as a simple and elegant arrangement. They have a much neater head, and the choice of varieties is growing every year.

The narcissi, when placed full-face forward in an arrangement, can dominate too much, so it is preferable to turn them in a free-form arrangement like this one.

Cattails grow wild by water, and they have a natural, yet sculptural, look. They are becoming increasingly popular in floristry, and the tallest are great in big vases – they have an excellent line as well as still being rather unusual. According to superstition, they are unlucky – but I'm certainly not going to listen to that!

Bear grass is excellent for giving any arrangement dimension and softens the hard edges of the vase.

We are all familiar with the many over-produced varieties of iris. They offer bright colors but don't last at all well. The bigger Dutch iris have stronger heads and last for a much longer time. They also have a wonderful natural wildness.

17

LILY CANDELABRA

This is a very special, elegant arrangement and one that needs quite a lot of forward planning! It uses a candelabra as its base, around the arms of which ivy, a growing plant, is trained to grow. The base of the candelabra and the ivy itself are both "planted" in a terracotta pot which has been half filled with soil for the ivy to grow. On top of this, I've put wet floral foam, which not only keeps the ivy alive, but gives sustenance to the cut flowers, too. The lilies and narcissi are arranged to follow the shape of the candelabra.

I've kept the terracotta pot in its natural state and simply decorated it with a bow, but you could paint it another color. The bases of the candleholders are lined with laurel leaves to give a teardrop effect. All in all, it makes a perfect special occasion arrangement for, say, a christening, where it could take pride of place in the center of the table.

WHAT YOU WILL NEED

In order of construction

- 1 flowerpot (9 inches diameter)
- 1 ivy plant
- 1 candelabra (18 inches span)
- Floral foam
- 3 candles
- 1 bunch (5) laurel leaves
- 7 'Casablanca' lilies
- 2 bunches narcissi

Compared to other lilies, 'Casablanca' lilies are expensive – but they're worth it. A single stem can carry anything from three to nine heads, so fortunately you don't need many! Sometimes, the stem is not strong enough to carry all these flowers, but you can give it support so it doesn't droop by tying a stick or cane to the stem. They open to a perfect white and have the most sensational bouquet.

The narcissi give a spring feeling – paperwhites or daffodils would work, too. Narcissi have a lovely scent, but bear in mind they might need replacing as they won't last so long as the lilies.

THE FLOWERPOT TREE

This arrangement is fun, but it takes a lot of preparation. Mix up enough quick-drying concrete to fill 4 inches, or half the depth, of the terracotta pot. While the concrete is still liquid place the stake in the center and keep it in place until the concrete has dried. At the top of the stake, place a large block of floral foam covered with chicken wire, using ordinary wire to tie it on. Once the concrete base has dried out, put two blocks of foam on top of it.

The flowers themselves are very simple – they have been turned into something rather more sophisticated and unusual by the style of the arrangement. Keep the flowers short to emphasize the shape of a tree – but aim for a natural rather than a tight topiary feel.

WHAT YOU WILL NEED

In order of construction

- 1 terracotta pot (18 inches diameter)
- 1 wooden stake (3 feet long)
- 1 small bag quick-drying concrete
- 3 feet chicken wire
- 3 large blocks floral foam
- 1 reel wire
- 2 bunches (10) viburnum foliage
- 5 bunches (50) Marguerite daisies
- 30 ranunculus

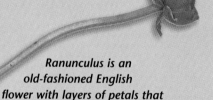

Ranunculus is an old-fashioned English flower with layers of petals that gradually open up. It's one of my favorites.

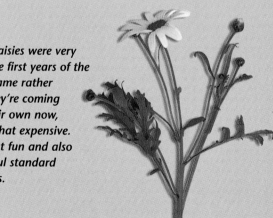

Marguerite daisies were very popular in the first years of the '90s and became rather overused. They're coming back into their own now, and are not that expensive. They are great fun and also make beautiful standard topiary plants.

Viburnum foliage has a fresh, natural spring feel, and lovely dark green leaves and buds that blend well with the flowers.

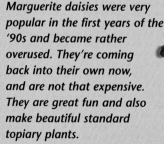

HAND-TIED SHEAF

This is a flat arrangement. It starts with the ficus foliage, laid out flat on the table in a fan shape. The flowers are layered flat on top of this. It is tied together with a raffia bow and, when it is untied, it can be simply lifted up and put straight into a vase – it is already arranged. This makes it a much better gift than the method of arranging flowers by size and wrapping them in cellophane – then the recipient has to dismantle all the layers and arrange them. It also shows the flowers off to their best possible advantage.

I've chosen spring flowers that have autumnal colors – rust-colored tulips, calendulas, and butterflyweed. If you want more springlike colors, go for bright yellows, such as daffodils, and blues, perhaps using crocuses, instead.

WHAT YOU WILL NEED

In order of construction

- 1 bunch (10–15) ficus foliage
- 20 butterflyweeds
- 9 tulips
- 9 calendulas
- 1 hank of raffia

You have to be very careful with calendulas; their stems snap easily. Strip the leaves off very gently and place them so they have support from the flowers around them.

Tulips came originally from Turkey. Taken to the Netherlands by Dutch merchant-adventurers, they have been associated with the Netherlands ever since. The Dutch are master flower growers and have developed an unbelievable range of strains and varieties, and are fast approaching the tulip-growers' Holy Grail of a perfectly black tulip.

Butterflyweed has a lovely fresh citrus scent, and its delicate sprays of flowers work beautifully in arrangements. It deserves to be better known than it is.

23

BLOSSOMS IN THE SPRING

This is a very simple arrangement – the last word in understated elegance. Its grace stems from the freshness of early spring flowering branches which are laden with buds and blossom. Flowering branches from the prunus family, such as apple or cherry, are perfect and give a slightly oriental feel, but you could use hydrangeas or forsythia from your backyard. Earlier still in the year, you could take pruned stems from your trees or shrubs with leaf buds on them, place them in water, and in a warm room, the leaves will open to reveal the freshest green imaginable. The arrangement serves as a caution that the simplest is often the best – florists can often make things too complicated.

WHAT YOU WILL NEED

In order of construction

- 1 weathered terracotta vase
  (6 inches diameter)

- 2 bunches (10) prunus flowering
  branches

- 5 cymbidium orchids

Cymbidium orchids are increasingly popular. They are sold by the stem – and each stem can have up to eighteen flowers. Cymbidium get their name from the Greek word for boat, cymbid – a reference to the boat-shaped petals.

Condition flowering branches from trees and bushes, such as these prunus stems, by splitting the stems and leaving them in lukewarm water for several hours before arranging. The arrangement would be equally successful with flowering branches used alone without any other flowers – the ultimate in delicacy.

VANITY FAIR

This free-standing arrangement makes a spectacular Valentine's Day surprise. I've chosen 'Red Lion' amaryllis instead of the more usual choice of roses for February 14 but kept to the heart-red color scheme, which is picked up in the burlap wrapped around the frame. The shape is built up gradually. Floral foam has been cut to shape and held in position with chicken wire; then the outline is made using the amaryllis as the tallest flowers. It is important to place these first since they have to be very firmly positioned – they have very heavy heads, especially when fully open, which puts a lot of pressure on their stems. When they are securely rooted in the foam, fill in the gaps with the foliage, followed by the veronica, then the tulips, and finally the guelder rose, or European cranberrybush – these give the arrangement depth and body.

This is an arrangement that will not only last but grow! The amaryllis open superbly, and the tulips will bend in their own directions. Keep the floral foam well watered since both these flowers drink a lot.

WHAT YOU WILL NEED

In order of construction

- 1 frame (4 feet high)
- 1 block floral foam
- 12 inches chicken wire
- 9 feet red burlap
- 9 'Red Lion' amaryllis
- 9 blue veronicas
- 20 red tulips
- 1 bunch (5) camellia foliage
- 5 guelder roses (European cranberrybush)

I have used blue veronica here, but white and lilac varieties are also available. You need to remove as many leaves as your arrangement will allow; otherwise, the water will go into the leaves and the flowers won't last. It is a particularly good structural flower for hand-tied arrangements.

The guelder rose is my absolute favorite flower. It can change just about any arrangement for the better, giving depth, filling gaps, and bringing contrast and interest. The ones used here are hothouse grown, but in many countries, it grows as a wildflower.

'Red Lion' amaryllis is an excellent variety of flower. It opens beautifully and last quite a long time.

Camellia foliage is exceptionally long-lasting with a good, glossy shine. You can also buy stems with flower heads and encourage them to bloom in a warm room.

Tulip growers have developed ever deeper shades of bloom. Here I have used the darkest red I could find to capture the romantic theme of the arrangement.

SPRING EFFERVESCENCE

Here, three remarkably different effects have been created from a combination of almost exactly the same flowers. The tall ones create a mini-garden effect with a loose, natural growing style. Alternatively, you can cut them very short for a highly structured look. In all these arrangements, you can simply rejoice in a burst of color.

WHAT YOU WILL NEED

In order of construction

(All three arrangements)

- Metal containers
- Floral foam
- Moss
- 3 guelder roses (European cranberrybush)
- 4 to 8 each of 2 or 3 varieties of tulip

(Center)

- ½ bunch (5) hyacinths
- 1 bunch (10) anemones
- 9 'Burrett' tulips

(Right)

- 9 French tulips
- ½ bunch (5) hyacinths
- 1 bunch (10) anemones
- 2 bunches (10) flowering branches of cherry

Moss gives a finished natural look and is excellent for hiding the foam beneath the stems.

White hyacinths have a lovely scent – though some people can find it over-powering, so don't put them on a dining table. They also come in pink and blue and, most recently, a yellow variety has been developed.

A COCKTAIL OF SPRING FLOWERS

This light terracotta container has been chosen to complement these lovely spring flowers – aiming here at the feeling of a fresh garden in spring. The hyacinths bring their delightful fragrance to the arrangement, while the mixture of blue with white gives the whole arrangement an elegant – even regal – look.

The dark-green foliage of the jasmine and butcher's broom gives a dramatic backdrop to the flowers, making them stand out even more. You are hit by the mixture of bright colors and strong scent the moment you enter any room this arrangement is in. It is an instant rush of spring – made to have extra zest by the mixture of guelder rose (European cranberrybush) and veronica!

WHAT YOU WILL NEED

In order of construction

- 1 terracotta container (8–10 inches diameter)
- 1 block floral foam
- ½ bunch (5) jasmine foliage
- ½ bunch (5) butcher's broom foliage
- 5 hyacinths of each color
- 10 veronicas
- 3 guelder roses (European cranberrybush)

Jasmine has a rich, dark-green foliage which is easy to work with, but which must be cut properly to maintain the fullness and dark effect.

Veronica comes in different shades of blue, white, and pink. For such a tiny flower, it has a lot of foliage. In fact, there is too much for its own good. Remove as much as possible before arranging it, or the leaves will steal the water and the flower will prove itself to be short-lived. With a clean stem it lasts well.

31

LIGHT SPRINGS FORTH

This arrangement can be used with or – as here – without candles.
The flowers are secured in floral foam inside the candle holders. If
you want to add the candles, simply add an extra candle cup and
pin it into the floral foam. You should always ensure that lighted
candles are never left unattended or in reach of children or pets.

Even without the candles to light it, this candelabra makes a
very dramatic statement as a pedestal arrangement. The flowers
used alone can be allowed to be a little wider than when candles are
used. The arrangement can also be adapted for a table, in which
case the flowers would be tighter and have a uniform length – that
way everyone can see each other across the table!

WHAT YOU WILL NEED

In order of construction

- 1 candelabra (18–24 inches span)
- Floral foam
- 6 x 3 inches florist's tape
- 2 bunches (10) butcher's broom
- 10 bright blue delphiniums
- 24 'Grand Prix' roses
- 12 guelder roses (European
  cranberrybush)

*The free-flowing
delphiniums let light
filter through while
showing their brilliant blue
color. The overall effect is
one of dazzling light.*

*'Grand Prix' rose is an excellent
variety. Here, it's used in bud, and
as it opens, the arrangement itself
will grow. People seem to have strong
opinions about using roses in flower
arrangements – the best advice is to invest in
a good quality rose and you should have no doubts
over the overall texture, longevity and movement as
they are guaranteed with a top quality rose.*

SUMMER

summer

This is the season of the greatest abundance for flowers. Not only are there more varieties of flowers around, they offer the widest color choice of the year, and they are, of course, at their cheapest – so this is the time to make the most extravagant arrangements of your imagination! Foliage is also at its best, so make the most of it.

Summer's vibrant colors – all those reds, yellows, oranges – make even the memory of winter seem far away. This is also a good time to mix and match – to try things out. There are all sorts of exotic flowers around, as well as lots of "country flowers" that have wild origins, such as sunflowers, bachelor's buttons, delphiniums, and sweet peas. If you live in the country and the more exotic flowers are not available, look around you for inspiration – you are surrounded with a huge variety of flowers and foliage. Herbs such as dill and fennel make wonderful "fillers" in an arrangement, and even "weeds" like Queen Anne's lace can look fabulously sculptural. Summer fruits – strawberries, blackberries, and grapes – add another dimension: they're good to eat if they're part of a table arrangement, too!

THE MILK CHURN

This arrangement is a mixture of classics. The milk churn is itself a classic design – and one that, after all, has never been bettered – yet with all the redolence of the countryside. The feature flower is the classic white arum lily – with nothing to beat it in terms of its height and stateliness. In fact, although the arum is considered rather a stylish and unusual flower, it grows happily in most places with a temperate climate, so it is as much at home in the country as the milk churn. Because it is such a strong flower, it is likely to takeover any arrangement, and here it is given full rein, with the accompanying flowers, twigs, and foliage in a supporting role.

In this container, this is an ideal arrangement for a country wedding, where it would make a beautiful and dramatic statement. In a stylish tall vase, it would be perfect for just about any grand occasion.

WHAT YOU WILL NEED
In order of construction

- 1 milk churn
- 5 stems kentia palm leaves
- 5 stems contorted willow twigs
- 9 variegated arum lilies
- 10 cotton bolls
- 1 bunch butcher's broom

The kentia palm leaves echo the exotic look of the arum flowers. Unlike the arum, the kentia really is a tropical plant, however. The leaves can be bought, but many people grow kentias as pot plants, and trimming off an occasional leaf to use in an arrangement will not harm their growth.

Cotton bolls are equally at home in water or in a dry container. If you have some with rather short stems, the arrangement need not look unbalanced. They can be placed without their stems in the water.

Willow gives height and presence to any arrangement.

Arum lilies bruise easily – developing unsightly black patches – so they must be treated gently. They can also become discolored around the edges of the petals, forming a brown fringe, which can be removed with scissors, however. If you cut off the damaged area, carefully following the shape of petals, the flowers will look as good as ever.

The butcher's broom has great curves and clean foliage. Look for a dark green color – a sure sign that it is healthy and will, therefore, last much longer.

39

THE CONTESSA'S BOUDOIR

This voluptuous, overblown arrangement has the look of a Mediterranean boudoir. In fact, it is made so it can hold a candle at its center and, as such, would be an excellent arrangement for a table at a wedding or a bar mitzvah. Fruit has become very popular as an intrinsic part of flower arrangements – and the fruit itself ends up being eaten!

This arrangement looks complicated and expensive, but the opposite is actually the case. It is really quite simple, and you can use washed fruit and flowers from your yard or buy whatever is in season. Just make sure you balance the colors and shapes of the fruit and flowers you choose.

WHAT YOU WILL NEED

In order of construction

- 1 wire basket (10 inches diameter)
- Floral foam
- 1 bunch (5) salal leaves
- 3–5 apples
- 2 bunches black and green grapes
- 1 bunch (10) pittosporum
- 20 'Toscani' roses
- 3 stems unripened dates

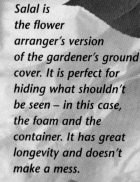

Salal is the flower arranger's version of the gardener's ground cover. It is perfect for hiding what shouldn't be seen – in this case, the foam and the container. It has great longevity and doesn't make a mess.

The pittosporum is a widely available foliage plant for arrangements. I chose it here because its rather delicate, variegated leaves soften the harder green of the salal and pull the shape together.

'Toscani' is a new rose – and an exceptionally successful one. It has become so popular because of its height (30–35 inches) and the large flower heads. Unlike some large-headed roses, which can be quite disappointing, 'Toscani' lasts very well, and the flowers open to reveal many different shades.

The combination of fruit was selected to enhance the 'Toscani' roses. I chose the unripened dates, in particular, to link the color of the roses with that of the foliage. Other color and shape combinations can work just as well.

41

HAND-TIED BOUQUET

This blue and yellow arrangement vibrates with the colors and flowers of summer, reminding me of a field of sunflower heads swaying in the wind and turning to face the sun. The sunflowers are mixed with a lovely bright blue cultivar of delphinium, which combines a lightness and fragility with vibrant color. The yellow calla lilies bring their own glorious sheen and deeply glowing color.

The arrangement has been done in a spiral shape for a loose, natural look, and can be popped into a vase ready-made. The wrapping is a blue Italian fabric paper that picks up the color. In fact, anything can be used to wrap up arrangements – not just cellophane. If it were tied more tightly, this arrangement could be carried as a bouquet.

Sunflowers and delphiniums are often regarded as garden flowers – or in the case of sunflowers, as crops – but they are used increasingly by flower arrangers nowadays.

WHAT YOU WILL NEED

In order of construction

- 1 bunch (30 strands) bear grass

- 9 sunflowers

- 9 yellow calla lilies

- 9 bright blue delphiniums

- 6 feet fabric giftwrap paper

The range of the delphinium family grows and grows – there are colors from the darkest hybrid blues through the lighter blues and even, nowadays, pinks. One of my favorites is this striking blue that is almost transparent. Like sunflowers, delphiniums should be cut with a knife, not clippers.

Sunflowers are very thirsty and need a long, diagonal cut made with a knife – not with shears – to enable them to drink as much water as possible. Take off all but a couple of the leaves, so they don't droop. If you have sunflowers with damaged petals, you can just remove them all! The seed head used on its own is equally interesting.

The yellow calla lily is a strong, classic flower. It has a vibrancy of color and a sheen that are breathtaking. It also has a beautiful furled shape – it's almost too perfect!

SCENT OF SUMMER

This frosted glass contoured vase looks good on a mantelpiece or a coffee table. The flowers are grouped to highlight each one individually, and the combination of whites and creams gives a feeling of the utmost light and delicacy, with just the slightest hint of blue from the miniature agapanthus. These are all – agapanthus, freesias, roses, jasmine – country flowers at heart, but grouped together in this way, they look much more sophisticated.

Perhaps the most important feature of this arrangement, though, is its scent. The three main flowers all have a heady fragrance and, mixed together, will fill the room with sweetness. Altogether, this is a perfumed blend of the best of summer.

WHAT YOU WILL NEED

In order of construction

- 1 vase (6 inches diameter)
- Floral foam
- Small bunch (5) butcher's broom
- 20 'Hollywood' roses
- 3 bunches white freesias
- 9 miniature agapanthus
- 5 stems jasmine

Agapanthus is usually a rather large flower, but here I have chosen the miniature version. This light blue gives just the right touch of color to this arrangement, but there are good dark blues, too.

Jasmine is my favorite for wedding bouquets. It not only looks lovely; it is also supposed to be therapeutic – its scent soothes and calms anxious brides.

The 'Hollywood' rose is a new one. It has a porcelain color, though without the hint of pink. It also has a good-sized head and lasts well.

Freesias come in many different colors, but in the hybridization to produce them, they can lose their scent. The white ones are used here for the intensity of their scent and the purity of their color.

45

A TROPICAL WALL ARRANGEMENT

More and more people are using walls for arrangements. It started in public buildings, such as restaurants, where they were used as "living" paintings. They give the opportunity of using both height and breadth and can look like a garden growing from the wall or, as here, can have a striking, exotic appeal. Nowadays, people are using this two-dimensional effect at home, too.

Heliconia is a very strong-looking tropical flower and can take over an arrangement. Here, it is used with the comparatively understated gloriosa lily, and between them, they achieve a perfect balance, showing off the best elements of tropical flowers.

WHAT YOU WILL NEED

In order of construction

- 1 hanging wicker basket with inside vase

- 3 stems Italian butcher's broom

- 3 stems heliconias

- 2 bunches (20) gloriosa lilies

The gloriosa lily is a fragile flower with a particularly delicate stem. For this reason, great care must be taken during transportation, when it must be protected from injury. Once arranged, the lovely, delicate blooms are very long-lasting.

Heliconia comes in a wide variety of colors, and it is becoming increasingly better known as people travel farther afield – although it is still sometimes confused with the bird of paradise flower, which could be substituted in this arrangement. Heliconia is on a grander scale – the flowers used here were cut down from a 6-foot stem – and new varieties are appearing constantly.

Cymbidium orchids have a very wide range of colors, the result, it is said, of being a "selfish" flower. When they are visited by bees, instead of providing nectar, these orchids take the pollen from the bee. Their multifarious colors may be a means of fooling the bees into thinking they are actually a different type of flower.

Lisianthus comes in many different colors and has become very popular in recent years. It is a very strong flower, often confused with an open rose.

SCULPTURED SHAPES

The idea behind these three arrangements is that sometimes certain flowers are strong enough simply to stand alone, rather than being mixed with other flowers where they may not be shown to their best advantage. This is certainly true of each of these flowers – nerines, lisianthus, and cymbidium orchids. They are all flowers that can be mixed with others, but on their own, they look even more stylish. Bear grass is added to give depth; otherwise, these are the simplest possible arrangements, reminiscent of Japanese *ikebana*, where flowers are used much more sparingly, often as single stems.

The simplicity of the arrangement is given extra interest by these unusual contemporary stainless steel and frosted glass vases. The vases are lifted slightly off the ground, which gives extra height, and the three used together would make a stylish arrangement for an entrance hall or a special function.

WHAT YOU WILL NEED

In order of construction

- 3 frosted glass vases (3 sizes)
- 2 bunches (30 strands) bear grass each vase
- 5 stems cymbidium orchids
- 9 lisianthus
- 9 nerines

Nerines come in a choice of colors, from vibrant pinks to the red used here. They are excellent value and very long-lasting. Buy blooms that have a small leaf just beneath the flower. You should remove this just before you arrange the flowers; otherwise, they will wither.

CORAL REEF

This is an arrangement that shows how you can turn a boring large plain glass vase into an interesting one! In this case, there is an inner vase which is narrower and shorter to hold the flowers, while the main vase is filled with the treasures from a sea bed, bought at a reputable supply store. There are shells, some green seaweed or seagrass (beach grass), a starfish, and a shell with an orchid peeping out. Given the theme, the flowers in the arrangement must, of course, be tropical. The feature plant is ginger, mixed with shoots from the tresene plant and bear grass.

The overall effect of this arrangement is sculptural, but the idea can be translated into just about any theme. For a children's party, you could team a container full of candy and jelly beans with the sorts of flowers children love, such as sunflowers and daisies.

WHAT YOU WILL NEED

In order of construction

- 1 inner glass vase (3 inches diameter)
- 2 bunches (10 strands) seagrass (beach grass)
- 1 bunch (30 strands) bear grass
- 3 ginger flowers
- 3 ginger leaves
- 2 bunches (10) tresene shoots
- 1 outer glass vase (6 inches diameter)
- 10 oyster shells
- 1 pink cymbidium orchid
- 5 starfish

Ginger flowers come in two different colors, red and light pink. Ginger stems and leaves can be up to 5 feet tall. Ginger is becoming increasingly available, and even one stem can make a strong statement in an arrangement.

The tresene belongs to a large family and has various colors, from the two-tone green used here to dark purples. They are more commonly known as houseplants, but the shoots are excellent in arrangements and have great longevity.

WATERING CAN

Many people feel arrangements belong in vases or bowls specially designed for the purpose. In fact, you can use a container effectively if you think about which flowers will best match it. In this case, a watering can – that most everyday container – is teamed with gerberas as the basis for a fun arrangement.

Vegetables are being used more and more frequently in contemporary floristry. In this case, I have picked the dark purple cow's tongue cabbage to link with the alliums and contrast with the bright yellow gerberas and the cerise celosia.

WHAT YOU WILL NEED

In order of construction

- 1 watering can
- 7 cow's tongue cabbage
- 11 gerberas
- 9 *Celosia venezuela*
- 20 alliums

Celosia venezuela is quite a small variety compared to most of this family. The larger ones are also lovely, but their heads are very heavy; and this variety was chosen to be in scale with the gerbera. They have a rhubarblike stalk, and it is very important to remove the leaves quickly or the stem will get mushy.

Cabbages are now specially grown for floristry – they are allowed to bolt so they have especially long stalks. Unfortunately, they don't last much more than a day or two, and they can smell horrible! This one, cow's tongue, lasts better than most, but it can still be removed to give the rest of the arrangement a new lease on life.

The gerbera will last well if conditioned properly. Cut the stems on a slant and let them have a first drink while they are still wrapped in paper so that their heads stay straight. If they have this first drink with their heads crooked or drooping, they will stay that way when you try to arrange them and never pick up. The cold has a similar effect on them, so keep them out of drafts.

THE ROSE TOPIARY

These urns originate in China, where they are produced with a shiny, metallic finish. They then make their way to The Netherlands, where the Dutch transform them by burying them in the ground to age them quickly. (They are then sold at double the price!) They are, of course, a classic shape and particularly suited to formal arrangements.

I've chosen a topiary shape for these roses to give a regal look. Roses come from such a huge family, it is difficult to know where to begin to choose. Here, I have simply chosen two of my favorites, each one special for a different reason. The salal leaves are used as an integral part of the arrangement, and they can also be turned over to show the pattern of their veins.

WHAT YOU WILL NEED

In order of construction
(For each urn)

- 1 rusted urn, lined with plastic

- Floral foam

- 3 bunches (15) salal leaves

(Opposite left)

- 40 'Grand Gala' roses

(Opposite right)

- 40 'Oriental Curiosa' roses

'Oriental Curiosa' is a very new rose. Terracotta, large-headed, and long lasting, it shows movement as it opens. It has been developed by the grower who produced the Leonardis rose and will prove as popular.

'Grand Gala' is one of my favorite roses – and there are many red roses to choose from. This one starts small-headed and develops into what most florists feel is the perfect rose shape. It has a velvety texture, too, and is very long-lasting.

SUMMER TRUMPET

A trumpet-shaped vase is ideal for this type of flower arrangement. It has a sturdy base and an open top for great width, while its narrow center holds the flowers firmly.

Ginger is an exotic and tropical flower, while delphiniums are redolent of summer from altogether milder climates. Yet they work together beautifully. Although they have entirely different characters, they are both strongly architectural flowers. Like the delphiniums, the lilac is the lightest of flowers, yet has a jewellike color.

WHAT YOU WILL NEED

In order of construction

- 1 vase (8–10 inches diameter)
- 1 bunch (5) butcher's broom
- ½ bunch (5) salal foliage
- 9 red ginger flowers
- 7 delphiniums
- 3 dracaena
- 7 lilac

If treated and used correctly, ginger flowers are one of the longest lasting – and certainly one of the most exotic flowers you can use to add an extra dimension to an arrangement.

Lilac's woody stem needs to be split before arranging so the water can reach its head. Unfortunately, nowadays florist's lilac is usually forced and so probably lacking its wonderful scent – unless you grow your own.

FALL

fall

Autumn paints with a golden palette. This is a time of yellow and orange montbretia or bronze and golden gerberas. There are still sunflowers around, too, while foliage reinforces the palette and adds deep purples. The other new element for fall arrangements comes from the theme of the harvest. This is the time to introduce masses of fruit and, in particular, vegetables as sources of inspiration, color, and texture. Pumpkins, pomegranates, and gourds give a voluptuous feel to arrangements – and remember the New England effect of mixing chrysanthemums and pumpkins. Consider, too, traditional harvest themes – wheat and barley can be used both fresh or dried. This is also the time of many festivals that form the themes of great arrangements – think of Halloween and Thanksgiving and other harvest-home celebrations.

PUMPKIN PARTY

The chrysanthemum family is enormous, but it is not usually one of my favorites for the simple reason that it suffers from overuse. You can find chrysanthemums at any time of year, but the fall is their real season; and if you look for them, there are some lovely varieties available. The 'Santini' has a small, delicate head and is sometimes known as the "rich man's chrysanthemum" – and it does cost a little more than the usual kind, but it's definitely worth it. The other variety is the 'Kermit' chrysanthemum – called after the famous puppet character frog because of its color!

The pumpkins have been hollowed out, lined with plastic and filled with a floral foam block to make them into containers, and are great fun for a Hallowe'en party.

WHAT YOU WILL NEED

In order of construction

All three arrangements

- 3 pumpkins
- 3 blocks floral foam

(Opposit left)

- 3 bunches (30) 'Santini' chrysanthemums

(Opposite right)

- 3 bunches (30) 'Kermit' chrysanthemums

(Opposite center)

- 9 peppers
- 9 gonipuricarpus
- 9 pyracanthas

Pyracantha is another well-shaped branch that children really like the look of.

Both 'Santini' and 'Kermit' chrysanthemums are great fillers and have been arranged to follow the natural domed shape of the pumpkin.

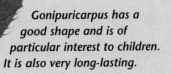

Gonipuricarpus has a good shape and is of particular interest to children. It is also very long-lasting.

63

PARTY PLANTER

The idea of this arrangement is to use an existing – growing – planter that you already have at home and give it a new look by adding extra flowers. Here, the existing plants are guzmania and cordyline, so I've added exotic flowers to match them. But it doesn't really matter what they are; you can use the same technique to make it more interesting. Most houseplants are grown just for their foliage – not the case here, in fact – but whatever they are, extra flowers will spice them up for special occasions. The message is – use what you have.

Naturally, the cut flowers will not last in ordinary soil, so you need to put floral foam on top and wire it into the soil very carefully so you don't damage the growing plants. Cover the foam with reindeer moss.

WHAT YOU WILL NEED

In order of construction

- 1 rusted metal planter (12 inches diameter)
- 3 guzmania
- 1 cordyline
- 1 block floral foam
- 2 handfuls reindeer moss
- 3 oriental pineapples
- 10 Singapore orchids
- 5 cymbidium orchids

Baby oriental pineapples are bright and cheerful, and very effective in giving a tropical look to arrangements. Don't be tempted to eat them, though – they're very bitter!

There are two kinds of orchids used here. The Singapore orchid has a smaller head, jazzed up by its tiger stripes.
The cymbidium orchid (left) comes in multiple colors and has a lovely, large head.

The guzmania is a tropical plant from the bromeliad family and is excellent for adding color.

65

HAND-TIED FALL BOUQUET

Many people find that the fall makes them feel sad and nostalgic as they watch the leaves drop. For me, though, it is a wonderful season because I love its bronze and orange colors – they have a glowing brilliance unique to this time of year. I find the gorgeous colors of this bouquet evocative of autumn.

It is arranged in a spiral of stems, all of them cut quite short, so it would make a lovely wedding bouquet tied with a hank of raffia or could just as easily be placed in a large-mouthed vase. It is grouped to emphasize the individual flowers. Although forsythia is a traditional spring flower, its bright yellow is valuable as a good contrast to the other colors, and helps to light up the arrangement. The more traditional, darker autumnal oranges and browns would get lost on a dark day.

Chili peppers give great shape and color to the bouquet and are very long-lasting.

WHAT YOU WILL NEED

In order of construction

- 1 bunch (5) butcher's broom
- 1 bunch (5) grevillea
- 1 bunch (10) laurestinus
- 20 orange roses
- 1 bunch (10) forsythia
- 2 bunches (10) chili peppers
- 1 hank of raffia

Orange roses are perfect for a sunless fall day – used for a wedding bouquet, they'd show up beautifully in photographs.

I've used a combination of foliage. The grevillea is similar to the forsythia in color, while the laurestinus is a contrast and one of my favorite foliages.

Unlike its garden counterpart, floristry forsythia – which is grown specially in hot-houses for floristry use – has straight stems and no leaves. The buds will open to give a bright, sharp yellow.

FRUITS OF THE FOREST

This is a striking arrangement for an entrance hall. It stands about three feet high and on a pedestal would make an even stronger statement. This arrangement also shows how important the choice of vase can be. The same contents in a plain glass vase could look very ordinary, but the colored glass set in a metal frame with its gothic look makes the arrangement much more interesting.

The flowers and other contents of the vase are easily found in the yard or, indeed, the forest. The whole arrangement could have come from an autumn woodland but to a city eye it seems quite exotic.

This stylish arrangement could be made even more sophisticated by using blue delphiniums with orange hybrid or calla lilies. Or, a more rustic look could be achieved by adding a piece of driftwood around the base of a plain vase.

WHAT YOU WILL NEED

In order of construction

- 1 blue gothic vase (9–12 inches diameter)
- 1 bunch (5–10) beech twigs
- 1 bunch (5–10) twigs covered with lichen
- 1 bunch (5–10) cotoneaster
- 13 'Leonardis' roses
- 5 artichokes
- 9 rudbeckia
- 9 hypericum

The 'Leonardis' rose is a perfectly autumnal terracotta orange. It is quite a new variety, but already established as a big favorite among florists around the world. It is a hybrid (so without a scent), but it both opens and lasts very well. Each year its color seems to change slightly in tone, becoming an increasingly paler terracotta.

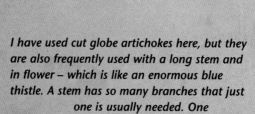

I have used cut globe artichokes here, but they are also frequently used with a long stem and in flower – which is like an enormous blue thistle. A stem has so many branches that just one is usually needed. One precaution – change the water frequently or it will start to smell horrible!

TERRACOTTA TOWER

In this arrangement, I've used two pots of the same size with a smaller one for the top. However, you could use three of different sizes with the smallest at the top of the stack. Each pot is lined and filled with floral foam. In order to create this staggered-stack effect shown here you will need pots with two or three holes in the base so that you can push a stick through alternate holes. To secure the stack so that it will stay steady when moved, push the top and center pots into the floral foam of the pot it sits on.

The fun feeling of this arrangement is reflected in the flowers themselves. Gerbera is a cheerful flower and available in a wide variety of colors, both with and without an "eye." This is an ideal table arrangement for a joyful occasion. Children, in particular, love these flowers. You could use roses, chrysanthemums, or virtually anything from your back yard in the same way.

WHAT YOU WILL NEED

In order of construction

- 3 terracotta pots (6 inches diameter)
- 3 pot liners
- 3 blocks floral foam
- 1 stick, approximately 18 inches long
- 3 handfuls spaghnum moss
- 1 bunch (20–30) rhododendron leaves
- 20 gerberas

Gerberas are available all year round. Group them by color for the best effect. They have a perfect shape and give any arrangement a good line. Their colors have a true gaiety, and they work just as well in an ordinary vase – but always try to use them in a full group to show them at their best.

The rhododendron leaves used here are a contrast to the gerberas, with their dark green gloss. Laurel leaves could be used equally well, or, the lime-green leaves of lady's mantle.

FALL CENTERPIECE

This is a real harvest arrangement using the produce and colors of the fall to great effect. It shows that you don't need to spend a fortune on expensive flowers and vases – you can use what you have in the kitchen and the yard. Here, a piece of driftwood gives the basic shape – this has a lovely sculptural look and is always a conversation piece. The uncooked red, green, and yellow bell peppers are cut in half, hollowed out, and used as containers. They are particularly effective because of their bright, contrasting colors.

The candles add a magical effect — but you must be sure never to leave lighted candles unattended or where children or pets may be able to reach them.

WHAT YOU WILL NEED

In order of construction

- 1 piece driftwood (18 inches long)
- 1 bunch lichen
- 3 red, green, and yellow bell peppers
- 1 branch beech leaves
- 3 stems red, green, and yellow floristry peppers
- 12 chili peppers
- 15–20 calendulas
- ½ lb chestnuts
- 3 candles secured with wire ties

These "floristry" peppers are grown purely for decoration – they are not edible.

Chili peppers can give a wonderful exotic feel to an arrangement like this, but you must be careful not to leave it where children or pets can reach.

I've used yellow calendulas instead of the more usual orange to give a lovely touch of brightness. Calendulas are a happy flower, whatever color you use. They are held naturally in the water inside the peppers.

BRILLIANT MOSAICS

This vase is made of different colored pieces of glass and picks up the rich colors and textures of the flowers used. This is a sophisticated combination of flowers and foliage, but they are arranged very loosely. Many arrangements are packed far too tightly, but in this case I've kept the flowers free enough to have some room to breathe – and these are ideal flowers for this technique. The poppies choose their own position, and the roses have the space to open fully. The butcher's broom is a perfect foil for the euphorbia – they have the same line but different colors.

Interestingly, poppies used alone would look equally exotic and beautiful in this vase, for a simpler arrangement.

WHAT YOU WILL NEED

In order of construction

- 1 mosaic vase
- 1 bunch (5–10) butcher's broom
- 20 'Grand Prix' rose
- 2 bunches (20) Iceland poppies
- 9 red *Euphorbia fulgens*

Euphorbia is a big family with a great variety of colors. Here, I've used a jewellike red. Always remember when using euphorbia that it is a very poisonous plant – the story is that it was once used for the poisonous tips of arrows. Always wear rubber gloves when handling euphorbia as it causes an allergic reaction in many people.

The dark red 'Grand Prix' rose is a brilliant, velvet-textured, dark red and opens like a perfect garden rose with its head held high. It is an old variety and tends to be rather expensive – but it's worth it.

Iceland poppies are often yellow, but I've used orange ones here to fit with the reds. They should never be allowed to drink too much or the stems wobble and die. They drink quite enough through the tiny hairs on their stems, so to prevent them from drinking from the bottoms of the stems, burn the ends to seal them.

Papyrus is very eye-
catching and a great
filler. It also lasts well
with only one
particular drawback –
it doesn't like dry heat,
so keep it away from
radiators and out of
direct sun.

This preserved moss is unusual as
it both holds its color and it
doesn't smell – many mosses are
quite smelly and prone to become
flaky after a week or so. This
variety holds its moisture well.

CAGED BIRDS FLY

The strelitzia is also known as bird of paradise and comes from the Canary Islands. It is a curious mixture of the exotic and the simple. In this arrangement, the leaves are used, too, to great sculptural effect, and the overall feel is that of birds about to take flight. The strelitzia used here has wonderfully long leaves and stems – in fact, these came from Italy which, at this time of year, produces the best version of this plant, as opposed to those from The Netherlands which are much shorter.

Papyrus is a great filler and very eye-catching in any arrangement, providing another sculptural element. The orange and green contrast makes this an even more striking piece, ideal for a tall table or stand. The angular positioning of both flowers and leaves is held tightly in floral foam, which is itself hidden beneath the lime-green moss.

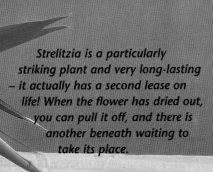

Strelitzia is a particularly striking plant and very long-lasting – it actually has a second lease on life! When the flower has dried out, you can pull it off, and there is another beneath waiting to take its place.

WHAT YOU WILL NEED

In order of construction

- 1 small bird cage (9 inches high x 4 inches wide)
- ½ block floral foam
- 2 handfuls lime-green preserved moss
- 9 strelitzias (with leaves)
- 5–7 papyrus stems

PARADISE CAPTURED

Here a structure has been used as an inspiration – in this case, it is the rails of a bar but could just as easily be the railings of a hallway staircase. These rails enclose the vase in a confined space and the "bird of paradise" strelitzia flowers peep out between the bars. The color of the vase is picked up by the guelder roses (European cranberrybush), which also adds its free-flowing effect. The dark-blue monkshood gives a good color contrast.

Always bear in mind where your arrangement will be placed and try to suit it to its position. A bar or a hallway, for instance, are quite busy areas, and the flowers used here are light and loose to reflect that. The arrangement can't be too wild or the flowers would get in the way. Here height rather than width is the order of the day. It is also rather a modern-looking location, and guelder roses (European cranberrybush) and "bird of paradise" fit perfectly due to their architectural style.

WHAT YOU WILL NEED

In order of construction

- 1 vase (6–8 inches diameter)
- 1 bunch (30 strands) bear grass
- 1 bunch (5) dogwood
- 1 bunch (5) butcher's broom
- 7 "bird of paradise" strelitzia flowers
- 7 monkshoods
- 5 guelder roses (European cranberrybush)

Strelitzia is such a striking looking plant that it can dominate an arrangement unless you take care to get a good balance of foliage and other flowers.

RUSTIC SUNSET

The container I've used here is an "aged" vase with a rusted effect. It is lined first with a waterproof liner; then the floral foam is cut into shape and placed inside. I've chosen it because it sets off the fall flowers beautifully. These vibrant colors would look good next to a roaring log fire!

The carthamus used here is fully open, but the eremurus is in bud. As the buds open, the arrangement develops – the buds open from the bottom of the stem up, like a tongue of flame – and gives it life. The montbretia, intertwined through the arrangement, almost looks like a flame itself, and the whole thing simply glows.

WHAT YOU WILL NEED

In order of construction

- 1 vase (8–10 inches diameter)
- 1 vase/pot liner
- Floral foam
- 1 bunch (5) grevillea foliage
- ½ bunch (5) salal leaves
- 7 eremurus
- 7 carthamus
- 10 montbretia

Carthamus comes in both orange and yellow. Cut the stems and place in water, checking that all the heads are healthy and remove any that are "droopy."

Grevillea adds a wonderful two-toned, wild effect.

WINTER

winter

You may find that the coming of winter means that the selection of flowers available to you is reduced slightly. Don't let this deter you, though! Instead, treat it as a challenge for your imagination. The dominant and most popular color of the season is easy to spot – red, red, red! Roses are particularly impressive in arrangements now, and the 'Red Lion' amaryllis is simply fantastic. It is great value and totally reliable. Holly offers a different dimension and is perfect mixed with white poinsettias.

You don't need to buy lots of flowers in winter, though. A few will go a long way – especially roses and 'Red Lion' or 'Hercules' amaryllis – when mixed with other elements. You can make all the difference with lichens, mosses, cones, and ordinary twigs, and foliage sprayed silver or gold. You can make it as exciting and dramatic as you want. Then, after all that red and melodrama, you come back to the freshness of spring as the seasons turn again.

ROCKET LAUNCH

This modern arrangement uses metal cones to give height to the calla lilies. In fact, under normal circumstances, the cones tend to be hidden, but here they are in full view to give a sculptural look – like a rocket about to be launched! In larger arrangements, the cones would be used to give height to flowers that are not tall enough in themselves and then be hidden among the other flowers.

The vase has been filled with floral foam, and the twigs, slate – particularly good against the metal – and moss are placed over it and wedged into place. The carnations give a strong line of color at the base, and the metal cones are then inserted at different angles, filled with water, and the lilies added. The dark red carnations and the almost-black callas give the arrangement the fiery feel of a takeoff.

WHAT YOU WILL NEED

In order of construction

- 1 metal vase (4 inches diameter)
- 1 block floral foam
- 2 handfuls lichen moss
- 1 bunch (5) lichen-covered twigs
- 3 broken slates
- 3 galvanized metal cones (10–12 inches long)
- 9 black calla lilies
- 9 red carnations

These dark red carnations are very long-lasting, and, like all carnations, they open perfectly every time. A carnation renaissance could be generated by the interesting new colors that are appearing nowadays – such as pistachio.

There are many different kinds of moss. Here, I've used lichen moss, which has a good color and makes an excellent contrast to the slate.

Calla lilies are almost too perfect in shape, color, and texture – and this could make them rather cold flowers. Here, I've used the moss and twigs to give them warmth and a more natural feel.

CHRISTMAS BOUQUET

Red-twigged dogwood is a wild plant in many countries and is used in this hand-tied bouquet to give an extra dimension. The stems have a wonderfully vibrant red color and, being extremely flexible, can be bent into just about any shape. Here, spirals of the plant have been looped dramatically into the bouquet. It can also be used as a protection for fragile plants that would otherwise be easily damaged. It gives the arrangement a most unusual shape, one that works equally well as a bridal bouquet or simply standing loosely in a vase. Either way, it is a very dark, simple, evocative bouquet.

The holly has been chosen for its rich green color. The ivy is not only part of the overall arrangement; it is also used to bind the stems. The lovely, resonant dark red of the 'Black Magic' rose makes this a particularly memorable bouquet.

WHAT YOU WILL NEED

In order of construction

- 1 bundle holly
- 1 bunch (5–10) red-twigged dogwood stems
- 20 'Black Magic' roses
- 1 bunch (5–10) trailing ivy stems

'Black Magic' roses have a lovely, velvety feel and open up beautifully with a good head – just as a rose should. 'Baccarola' with its very dark red color would be a good alternative. 'Grand Prix' also opens up and holds its shape well.

Red-twigged dogwood needs little attention when cut for an arrangement, and it lasts well. If it isn't available, willow would be a good alternative. The effect would be different because of the color, but it has the same suppleness.

CELEBRATION CANDLES

This is a tall arrangement with rich flowers – and it makes a real statement. It is particularly suitable for a celebration, such as a bar mitzvah or an anniversary, or for the entrance to a place of worship. Anchor floral foam onto the stand with tape and place the foliage to develop an outline, paying particular attention to the trail of ivy and eucalyptus. The 'Hercules' amaryllis are concentrated at the top to give breadth, with a few zigzagging down. The rosehips fill the gaps and the red tulips are grouped to give a truly sumptuous feel.

The arrangement would work more simply but just as effectively without flowers at all – the ivy could be draped around the candles and candelabra for a cool and elegant look.

WHAT YOU WILL NEED

In order of construction

- 1 church candelabra (6 feet tall)
- 1 block floral foam
- Florists' tape
- 1 bunch (5–10) ficus leaves
- 1 bunch (5–10) eucalyptus foliage
- 1 bunch (5–10) ivy stems
- 9 'Hercules' amaryllis
- 1 bunch (5–10) rosehips
- 20 dark red tulips
- 7 candles

'Hercules' amaryllis is one of my favorite flowers especially as they come in this glorious red color. These flowers will last for up to two weeks if the water is changed regularly – if not, the stem will get mushy and the flower itself will spoil.

Only the young foliage of the eucalyptus tree has this extraordinary shape and color. The mature foliage is much less interesting. It has a distinctive fresh, stimulating scent and dries out quickly – so make sure it has plenty to drink before you begin the arrangement. Then keep it well watered after it is in place.

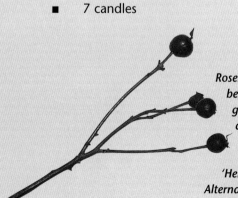

Rosehips often bear different-colored berries on the same stem, which gives a special interest to any arrangement. Here, their natural shape blends with the ivy while contrasting well with the dark 'Hercules' amaryllis and tulips. Alternatively, use berried ivy or blackberries.

THE GLACIER

This all-white arrangement was designed with a glacier in mind – so everything is the purest of whites, and the shape builds up to a jagged pyramid. The terracotta bowl has a wide mouth to give enough room to fit in both the candles and the floral foam for the flowers. The bowl was whitewashed to fit the color scheme. The candles are of different diameters and heights to reinforce the idea of the jagged edges of ice.

The flowers were chosen to give the coolest and freshest of looks. *Hellebores niger*, the Christmas rose, is an exquisite flower, while the paperwhites not only look beautiful – since they come from the narcissus family, they have a delicious scent, too. When the candles are lit, an even stronger fragrance is released.

WHAT YOU WILL NEED

In order of construction

- 1 white-washed terracotta bowl (6–8 inches diameter)
- 1 block floral foam
- 4 candles of different sizes
- 1 bunch (5) ming fern
- 1 bunch (5) butcher's broom
- 2 bunches (20) *Hellebores niger* (Christmas rose)
- 3 bunches (30) paperwhites

The hellebore family is an extensive one. The Christmas rose also comes in purple, and other varieties are very exotic – many of them are green. It is an expensive flower, but worth it since it lasts well despite its delicate looks.

Ming fern has an unusually soft feel – many ferns have rather prickly edges. It also has a good strong green color and covers a wide area easily.

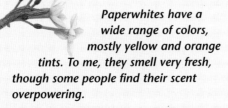

Paperwhites have a wide range of colors, mostly yellow and orange tints. To me, they smell very fresh, though some people find their scent overpowering.

GOLDEN ORNAMENTS

Here is another arrangement for the holiday season – this time an exquisite centerpiece for the table. It has a particularly neat shape since all the flowers have been cut short to follow the shape of the bowl, and each one can be seen in its own right with all the elements of the arrangement in balance. I have used a gold-colored fruit bowl, but you can use an ordinary ceramic one and simply spray it gold, as has been done with the leaves laid out on the table around the bowl. The broken bauble contains roses and gives the arrangement more reflective light as well as adding to its festive feel.

One of the nicest things about this centerpiece is its wonderful scent. The hyacinths have a very strong perfume and the pine and eucalyptus add their own distinctive fragrances. The walnuts offer a finishing festive touch.

WHAT YOU WILL NEED

In order of construction

- 1 gold ceramic bowl (12 inches diameter)

- 1 block floral foam

- 1 bunch (3) eucalyptus foliage

- 1 bunch (5) pine foliage

- 2 bunches (20) hyacinths

- 12 'Nicole' roses

- 6 walnuts

- 3 strands miniature gold stars

- 5 maple leaves sprayed gold

- 1 sprig mistletoe

- Gold-colored ornaments

I have used blue hyacinths here to contrast with the red of the roses. Like the roses, they open up so the arrangement changes and develops, and their scent is sensational.

'Nicole' roses are not scented, but are used here for their "frosted", wintry look. They last well and open up beautifully. They are a great favorite for winter bridal bouquets.

The fresh scents of the pine and eucalyptus complement the heady perfume of the hyacinths.

WINTER WONDERLAND

This is very much an arrangement for the holiday season. It combines all sorts of festive elements – berries, poinsettias, gold-sprayed foliage – and also has the great advantage at a busy time of lasting all the way through the holidays. I've used a glass vase in a metal frame that lifts it an extra four or five inches off the table. This means you can use standard-sized flowers and still get a big arrangement. It is a very classic style of arrangement – the flowers all face the front, so it would be ideal on a mantelpiece or in a foyer or hallway. I've emphasized the rather voluptuous, Greek amphora style of the vase by entwining the ivy around its base.

In this arrangement, I've sprayed birch twigs with gold paint to give a festive look, but virtually any foliage can be used and treated in the same way.

WHAT YOU WILL NEED

In order of construction

- 1 glass vase in a metal frame
- 9 winterberry branches
- 1 bunch (5–10) laurustinus
- 1 bunch (5–10) camellia leaves
- 7–9 'Hercules' amaryllis
- 1 bunch (5–10) birch twigs sprayed gold
- 7 poinsettias
- 1 bunch (5–10) trailing ivy stems
- 1 bunch (5–10) holly stems

The rich red of this 'Hercules' amaryllis is perfect used against the strong greens of the holly and ivy.

Everyone knows poinsettia as a houseplant, but it can also be bought cut for arrangements. Again, it has a very festive feel and is both inexpensive and long-lasting.

Winterberry is becoming increasingly popular in arrangements because it has masses of colorful berries. It has a good straight, woody stem and lasts for at least two weeks.

WINTER CANDLES

This is an unusual arrangement – it has a dark, even moody, look, due to its dark flowers, and when its candles are lit, it provides a wonderfully atmospheric centerpiece for the table. To me, it conjures up a mysterious, forgotten time when people would sit around the fire to tell stories in the flickering evening candlelight.

The candles are staggered to give different heights, and their light picks out the dark colors of the flowers and the oriental cabbages. The whole arrangement is set in floral foam but all the flowers – in particular the lilac – are large-headed, so the base is hidden easily. The purple lilac is beautiful, but unscented at this time of year when it has to be forced to flower. If you want the arrangement to have a fragrance, you could always use scented candles.

WHAT YOU WILL NEED

In order of construction

- 1 ceramic bowl
  (12 inches diameter)

- 1 block floral foam

- 1 bunch (5) viburnum foliage

- 1 bunch (5) laurustinus foliage

- 3 candles

- 5 ornamental cabbages

- 5 lilac stems

- 9 black calla lilies

I've used different shades of white and purple cabbages to create a contrast. Though these are already a popular plant for containers, they are only now starting to be cut for arrangements. Here, in floral foam, they last particularly well. If, however, you are putting them directly into water, you need to pick off the outer leaves first or they will turn brown.

Treated correctly, lilac lasts well. Split the stems and place them in tepid water for two to three hours. This way, they drink water quickly so it gets to the flower heads before the woody stems can seal themselves. They can then be arranged in the floral foam.

FRESH DECORATIONS

Everyone has a favorite way of decorating the tree at the holiday season. Some people like single-color balls, others prefer bows. Then again, some find lights and tinsel most appealing – while some of us like to put just about everything on the tree and hope for maximum impact!

Here, I've tried something a little more unusual – fresh decorations. The white poinsettias are plants growing inside their pots. The gerberas are cut flowers, secured in floral foam and placed in the pitchers, which themselves are miniature tankards. They can sit on a branch, held by the handle, or you can tie them on instead.

I've used poinsettias here because, for many people, they are the Christmas flower – though more often seen on a larger scale as potted plants. However, you could use open lilies, amaryllis, or roses. Then again, using red gerberas alone would make a stunning tree. I've sprayed the leaf gold, but it could be silver or any other color that appeals. Whatever you choose, living decorations will make a truly individual tree.

WHAT YOU WILL NEED

In order of construction

(Quantities based on making 15 decorations for a fir tree of 6 feet tall.)

- 15 rustic pitchers
- 3 blocks floral foam
- 15 eryngiums (thistles)
- 15 gerberas
- 15 white poinsettia plants
- 2 bunches bear grass, sprayed gold
- 2 bunches (15–20) asparagus leaves, sprayed gold

During the holiday season one can spray paint almost any foliage for a new effect. It is important to evenly spray the product for a more natural effect. Bear grass works really well.

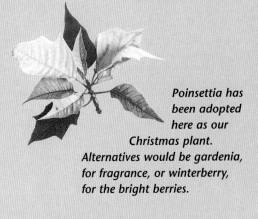

Poinsettia has been adopted here as our Christmas plant. Alternatives would be gardenia, for fragrance, or winterberry, for the bright berries.

JUDGMENT DAY

This arrangement has been designed very much to suit this unusual room. It is, in fact, an old courthouse, and the judge's bench and chair are still there – and are the most prominent features in the room. When you have something unusual like this, I think it's best to make the most of it.

The back of the seat itself forms a frame in which to place the arrangement. I've started by using long pieces of willow to form the outline. These are placed in a large container, and you can secure them either into floral foam or chicken wire. The willow is placed so the stems interlock and hold in place a second container. This is tied to the stems and secured. Flowers are put in the lower container to decorate the edge of the chair, while the second smaller container holds the flowers, such as the prunus flowering branches, that give height to the arrangement.

WHAT YOU WILL NEED

In order of construction

- 1 outer container (bucket) (12 inches diameter)

- Floral foam or chicken wire

- 5 willow twigs/branches

- 9 stems heliconia

- 1 inner container (bucket) (8–10 inches diameter)

- 7 kentia palm leaves

- 1 bunch (5) prunus flowering branches

The red heliconia used here sets off the wooden background. Heliconia comes in a wide variety of colors so it can be used to match many types of decor. If you cannot find heliconia you could use strelitzia "bird of paradise" instead.

Prunus flowering branches give the feeling that spring isn't so far away. They are very effective in arrangements because the buds open gradually. Be sure to split the stems well before arranging.

FLOWERS AFLAME

This arrangement is self-standing – it doesn't have a container. Simply tape the soaked floral foam securely to a tray so that it sits flat on the floor of a fireplace. Use the foliage to create the outline of your arrangement, working both on the upright and the horizontal ground level simultaneously, aiming to fill the opening of the fireplace. Next, you will need to cut lengths of wire to attach around each cone, leaving an 8–12 inch "tail" of wire. Then, position the gold twigs and the wired cones in a balanced formation against the foliage, inserting them directly into the floral foam. Place the pine foliage on the ground, as if it is overflowing from the fireplace. Now, add the leucadendrons.

For the finishing touch, randomly place cones and cinnamon sticks on the pine foliage, aiming to give it the feel of a forest floor. There should be no visible connecting line between the vertical and horizontal.

WHAT YOU WILL NEED

In order of construction

- 1 floral foam tray
- 3 blocks floral foam
- 1 yard florist's tape
- 1 bunch (5) grevillea foliage
- 20 cinnamon sticks
- 10 spiral twigs, sprayed gold
- 15 leucadendrons
- 3 branches/twigs of pine foliage
- 3–5 yards floristry wire
- 12 cones

To add a touch of wildness, randomly place the two-toned grevillea.

Festive goodies, such as cones, cinnamon sticks and spiral twigs, are ideal for winter arrangements – especially when sprayed in gold or silver. When selecting such items you should be very attentive of interesting shapes, size and forms.

Cinnamon sticks add a particular festive touch because the aroma wafts in the air and makes one think of warm biscuits and mulled wine.

TECHNIQUES & MATERIALS

EQUIPMENT

Before starting on any arrangement, check that you have all the right tools for the job. Arrange tools in the order that you will need them. This will help you to relax and concentrate. With flowers, as with most things, confidence is the key.

A good sharp knife is needed for conditioning. Cut sappy stems – such as sunflowers and delphiniums – with a clean slanting slice with as large a surface as possible so the flowers will drink well.

Plant food is used to keep the water pure by delaying the build up of bacteria which is what causes the break-down of the consistency of stems.

Shears are used for woody stems and foliage where scissors are unsuitable. They are particularly good for such blooms as lilac and roses.

Choose scissors that feel comfortable in your hand. They must be very sharp – if you are an artist, scissors are your paintbrush!

Chicken wire is useful to contruct a form around floral foam so that longer-stemmed flowers and foliage are supported well. You should choose a gauge that will fit the thickest type of stem in your arrangement.

Wires come in many different thicknesses, and it's important to use the right wire for a flower – too heavya wire will break it. As a rule of thumb, light wire is for flowers like freesia; roses need a medium wire; and woody stems should have a thick-gauge wire.

Use good-quality floral foam. It may cost a little more, but it's worth it. It won't disintegrate in the water, and it will hold flowers firmly in place.

Raffia is a good alternative to ribbon. Use it to tie bouquets and for a natural bow.

Floral tape is used to cover the wire and stem for boutonnieres.

Keep floral tape clean. Choose good strong tape for better holding power.

Good-quality ribbon adds to a formal bouquet. Choose the ribbon color by picking out the color of one of the flowers.

Twine is good for holding stems firmly in place and for making bows when using ribbon would be too formal for the choice of flowers in an arrangement.

Pins are used to fix fabric wrapping in place. They are also used to pierce the base of a tulip bloom where it meets the stem as this keeps the tulip head from drooping.

Candles add the extra dimension of light. Choose ones that burn without soot or drips. Always ensure lighted candles are never left unattended.

Wire is invaluable when making garlands or for invisibly attaching flowers to foliage arches or other structures.

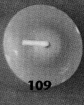

CONTAINERS

The choice of a container is crucial to an arrangement. A container can enhance your theme, be interesting in itself, or give a highly individual and refreshing slant on an arrangement. Don't just go for vases – all kinds of objects from old milk churns to an ordinary glass beaker can work.

One vital point on containers. They must always be properly lined; otherwise, you could cause water damage to the surface they are placed on, as well as ruining the flowers, which will dry out and die.

Extensions, such as these metal cones, are used to give short-stemmed flowers height while allowing them their own water source.

Use floral foam to create a tree shape – but always be careful to ensure that the container is properly weighted to support the tree construction you are forming.

Galvanized steel is suitable for repeated use and lends itself to all styles.

Terracotta and ceramic containers are ideal for simplistic arrangements or for an overall natural-effect.

Tall pasta jars (left) and vases in stands (below) are ideal for a table centerpiece so that the flowers sit above people's heads.

Commercial topiary frames can be expensive but are very effective – especially if you are not keen to try to make a frame yourself out of stong tensile wire, which can be difficult to form into the correct shape if you are not used to it.

This basket is lined with cellophane to avoid leakage. The stones are used to hold the cellophane in place and to act as drainage if soil and plants are added.

Wire containers used on their own can look harsh, but when lined with moss it gives a softer feel and tone between the flowers and the container.

You can create topiary shapes out of a floral foam base. For small topiary shapes it is often better to use a floral foam shaped base rather than a frame.

BASICS:

Preparing and Caring for Your Flowers

The techniques shown here and on pages 120–125 let you in on some tricks of the trade that will ensure that you keep your arrangements at their best so that you are able to enjoy your flowers fully. The techniques are all quite simple to do if you follow the instructions. They may sound basic, but they are essential to the success of your arrangements — if you don't get the basics right, the finished arrangement will suffer.

The first thing you should decide before starting an arrangement is how the final result will be displayed; fixed in floral foam in a container, loose in a vase, or formed into a bouquet. Once you have decided on the form your arrangement will take then you will be able to select the most suitable flowers and foliage.

The most important part of any arrangement is the preparation of the flowers and foliage which involves preparing stems (right) and conditioning flowers correctly, as described here and on the chart on pages 114–117.

PREPARING STEMS

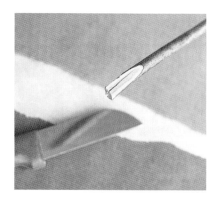

PREPARING
All flowers must be properly conditioned before arranging if you want them to last well. Woody stems must be split with a sharp diagonal cut and given a good, long drink. Medium woody stems, like roses, also need a diagonal cut and should drink lukewarm water. All foliage should be removed from the part of the stem that will be in water; otherwise, it becomes smelly and the arrangement won't last.

CONDITIONING ANEMONES
If anemones droop or wilt after a few days in an arrangement, take them out and recut the stems. Immerse them completely in water and they should revive to complete freshness. This trick works well for lilac, too.

Caring for Your Flowers

Certain kinds of flowers require special treatment and more conditioning than others — but it is always worth taking a little time before you start your arrangement, as your flowers will look better and last longer, too. Sunflowers, for instance, need a long slanted slice across the stem and an hour to drink, while lilac stems should be split and placed in lukewarm water for an hour. All flowers should have any foliage that will otherwise be in the water removed — leaves that are left on the stem will rot and make the water smell, as well as shortening the life of your flowers.

CONDITIONING

CONDITIONING ROSES
When you get your roses home, don't unwrap them if they are tightly wrapped already. If they aren't, rewrap them so that they are held straight. Let them drink cold water for at least two hours, cutting their stems with a good clean cut at a slant to take in water. This will prevent the common problem of roses nodding and dropping their heads.

CONDITIONING GERBERA
Gerbera are always thirsty – and they have a tendency to drink too much water for their own good. If they're put in deep water, they will overdrink and their heads will get too heavy and droop. To prevent this, always put gerbera in shallow water.

Flower Chart

Here are some of the most recurrent flowers in the book – organized under family name.

FLOWER	HEIGHT	SCENT	COLOR	FOLIAGE
AMARANTHACEAE CELOSIA	20–40in	—	various	coarse
AMARYLLIDACEAE AMARYLLIS	28–36in	—	various	—
NARCISSI	8–20in	strong, sweet	white, yellow	swordlike
NERINES	16–24in	chocolatelike	red, orange	—
APIACEAE ERYNGIUMS	20–28in	—	blue	thistlelike
ARACEAE ARUM LILIES	36in	—	white, variegated	—
CALLA LILIES	24in	—	various	—
ASTERACEAE CALENDULAS	12–20in	—	orange, yellow	long, thin, green
CHRYSANTHEMUMS	20–28in	—		soft green
GERBERAS	20–28in	—	various	—
MARGUERITE DAISIES	16–24in	—	yellow, white	carrotlike
SUNFLOWERS	20–40in	—	yellow, orange	large, heart-shape
CARYOPHYLLACEAE CARNATIONS	20–28in	—	various	long, thin; nodule-like stem joints
EUPHORBIACEAE EUPHORBIAS	20–28in	—	orange, white, yellow, red, pink	soft, dark green
POINSETTIAS	16–32in	—	red, white, pink	soft, dark green

WHAT TO LOOK FOR	IMMEDIATE CARE	LONG-TERM CARE	LIFE SPAN
clean, dry stems	strip foliage, cut stems	cut stems every 2 days, change water	7–10 days
stems aren't squashed	cut with scissors, put in water	change water regularly	2 weeks
dry heads, green stems	cut stems, place in water	recut stems, change water	1 week
clean, dry heads	cut stems, place in water	recut stems, change water	7–10 days
stems aren't brown	cut stems, put in water	change water	2 weeks
unmarked heads	cut with scissors, put in water	recut stems, change water regularly	2 weeks
unmarked heads	cut with scissors, put in water	change water regularly	2 weeks
clean, dry stems	strip foliage, place in water	recut stems, place in water	1 week
clean, dry stems, no yellow leaves	strip foliage, cut stems	change water, recut stems	weeks
fresh heads	support heads, place in shallow water	recut stems, change water	7–10 days
green leaves (not yellow), unbroken heads	strip foliage, place in water	recut stems, change water	1 week
heads unsquashed, dry stems	strip foliage, slice with knife	re-slice stems, change water	7–10 days
unbroken stems, strong heads	cut with scissors, put in water	change water regularly	weeks
no brown in flowers	wear rubber gloves, strip foliage, hold under running water until "milk" stops, wash hands	recut stems, change water	1 week
unbroken heads and stems	treat as euphorbia		1 week

	FLOWER	HEIGHT	SCENT	COLOR	FOLIAGE
	HYACINTHACEAE HYACINTHS	8–12in	strong, sweet	white, pink, blue, yellow	sword-shaped leaf
	IRIDACEAE FREESIAS	16–28in	sweet	various	—
	IRISES	20–28in	—	purple, white, yellow, black	sword-shaped leaf
	LILIACEAE LILIES	20–40in	strong, sweet	various	
	TULIPS	12–20in	—	various	sword-shaped
	MUSACEAE HELICONIAS	20–40in	—	various	—
	OLEACEAE FORSYTHIA	20–40in or more	—	yellow	—
	JASMINES	12–28in	sweet	yellow, white	
	ORCHIDACEAE ORCHIDS	12–32in	perfumed	various	—
	PAPAVERACEAE POPPIES	16–24in	—	red, orange, white	—
	RANUNCULACEAE ANEMONES	16–20in	—	red, white, purple, cerise	—
	DELPHINIUMS	20–40in	—	white, blue, mauve, pink	attractive, lobed and dissected
	HELLEBORES	8–16in	—	white, green	leathery, dark green
	RANUNCULUS	12–20in	—	various	scant, soft green
	ROSACEAE ROSES	20–40in	strongly perfumed	various	green, serrated

WHAT TO LOOK FOR	IMMEDIATE CARE	LONG-TERM CARE	LIFE SPAN
clean, dry stems	remove foliage, wash stems	recut stems, change water	1 week
clean, dry heads, undamaged stems	cut stems, place in water	recut stems, change water	7–10 days
dry, undamaged heads	remove foliage, place in water	recut stems, change water	1 week
green stems, bright shiny leaves, heads unfrozen	strip foliage, place in water	recut stems, change water	10 days
clean, dry stems, unbroken heads with healthy shine	wash stems, cut, remove excess foliage	recut stems, change water	7–10 days
no black stains on stems	cut stems, place in water	recut stems, change water	2 weeks
closed buds	split stems, put in water	recut stems, change water	2 weeks
leaves bright green	strip foliage, place in water	recut stems, change water	1 week
no black stains on heads, strong stems	cut stems, place in water	recut stems, change water	1–2 weeks
strong heads, dry stems	burn ends of stems, place in water	change water	7–10 days
good strong stems	cut with scissors, put in water	change water regularly	1 week
heads aren't wet	slice stems with knife and place in water	re-slice, change water	1 week
fresh heads	cut stems, place in water	recut stems, change water	1 week
dry stems, unopened heads	strip foliage, cut stems	recut stems, change water	7–10 days
dry, clean heads, no brown on stems	strip foliage, slice stems with knife, place in lukewarm water	recut stems, change water	7–10 days

Ivy

Butcher's broom

Rhododendron

Grevillea

Bear grass

Foliage

Foliage plays an increasingly prominent part in modern floristry. Balance is all-important, though – you must match the foliage to the flowers appropriately. If you put delicate flowers with too heavy a foliage, the effect will be to swamp the flowers altogether. It's vital that the two complement each other.

Foliage should be the basis, the bare bones, of your arrangement. It determines the shape and shows you the best positions in which to place your flowers, as well as giving them depth and texture. Foliage can sometimes be as expensive as flowers, but you can make it go a long way with careful cutting – and one stem can produce three!

Eucalyptus

Ginger plant leaf

Variegated pittosporum

Viburnum

TECHNIQUES:

Foam, Wire & Bows

Floral foam is used to hold the flowers and foliage firmly in place. Once the foam has been soaked (right), you will need to make sure it is fixed into the container securely. When placing your flowers, be decisive! If you end up taking them out and replacing them a lot, the foam will be full of holes and won't give a firm hold. When making a topiary foam base, it is important to get the shape right before you start adding the foliage and flowers.

Flower arranging often requires wiring techniques. Some flowers need wire to stop their heads from drooping (opposite). Wiring is also used to fix ornamental pieces, such as candles, into an arrangement (see below).

A bouquet looks complete when finished off with a stylish bow, so the technique shown opposite will add a final professional-looking touch.

FLORAL FOAM

1 *Fill a bowl with water and place your block of foam in it.*

2 *Leave to soak for 100 seconds – and it's ready to use. But don't oversoak as the foam may start to crumble. Now you should be able to cut the foam into the required shape, if necessary.*

WIRING A CANDLE

  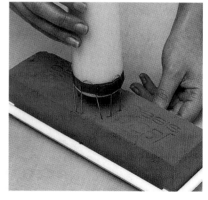

1 *Cut several lengths of wire in half and bend into a hairpin shape.*

2 *Use florist's tape (or masking or electrical tape – anything that's waterproof) to stick the hairpins around the base of the candle. Position the hairpins with half-inch gaps between them. Leave about 2 inches of wire below the candle.*

3 *Plunge the wire into the floral foam and the candle is secured. You can now build up your arrangement around the candle.*

WIRING FLOWERS

1 When you wire a flower to add support for the stem and head, you should take care to choose the right gauge of wire that will retain the flower's movement and make it look as natural as possible.

Insert the end of the wire into the base of the flowerhead carefully. Be sure not to damage the petals.

2 Gently twist the stem of the flower – not the wire – so that the flower spirals itself around the wire.

3 The wire doesn't need to be secured in any way – it stays in place by itself.

MAKING A BOW

1 Make a little twist in your ribbon – or twine or raffia – about 2 inches from the end. Make a loop and pinch it into the twist, holding it firmly between the thumb and index finger.

2 Make another loop opposite the first and tuck it under the thumb and index finger as before. Continue making loops on alternating sides. You can do as many as you like, but most florists prefer an uneven number – usually three loops above and two below.

3 Chop off the excess length of ribbon and use it to wrap around the center of the bow, tying it tightly behind. Pull out the bow to its fullest shape and tie around the bouquet over the twine.

TECHNIQUES:

Hand-tied Bouquet

This is so much more interesting and special than a flat arrangement. It is ready to put into a vase – you don't even need to untie it, as it's already arranged. Use at least two types of foliage; more leaf than flower can look better.

The preparation stage (step 1) is what takes the most time with a hand-tie – but you get a much better final result if you do prepare properly.

Using aquapacks, which hold a reservoir of water, means you can take an arrangement even on a long journey and, as it's filled with water, it will arrive as fresh as when it was first made. An aquapack is only really successful when you have short stems and plenty of them – a 12-inch bouquet is about the right size, and you must be sure it can stand up by itself before wrapping it up. The bow can go around the neck of the aquapack paper.

1 *After conditioning the flowers and foliage, strip the stems so there are no leaves at or below the tie point. This means that no leaves are in contact with water and the bouquet is not too thick to hold easily. Roses will need dethorning with a tool, such as a knife. For other types of stem it is easier to use your hands to strip the stems.*

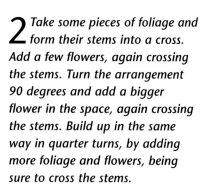

2 *Take some pieces of foliage and form their stems into a cross. Add a few flowers, again crossing the stems. Turn the arrangement 90 degrees and add a bigger flower in the space, again crossing the stems. Build up in the same way in quarter turns, by adding more foliage and flowers, being sure to cross the stems.*

3 *You should now have formed a spiral of stems which holds the flowers firmly in place and keeps the shape strong. When all of the flowers and foliage are in place, cut off the stems at a 45-degree angle. They should all be of the same length, except those in the center which should be a little shorter.*

4 *The narrowest point – the "neck" of the arrangement – is where you have been holding it. Tie the arrangement firmly at this point with twine. The arrangement should be able to stand up by itself on the table.*

MAKING AN AQUAPACK

1 *Take a square of cellophane and stand the flowers in the middle of it. Gather up the cellophane, pleating it in so it will be tight around the tie point and flare out just below the flowers.*

2 *Fill with water and tie very tightly with twine to prevent spillages.*

3 *When you receive an aquapack, pierce the cellophane to let out the water before you unwrap it.*

TECHNIQUES:

Topiary

You must be sure that you are clear about the shape you want before you start your topiary. Whether you are using moss or floral foam as a base, make sure you're completely happy about this underlying shape before you start adding flowers. There is a lot of choice in terms of shape and most things will work – round, oval, square, spiral. For spirals, it is vital that you create an even, uniform shape. For topiary trees, make sure the floral foam is very firmly secured to the "trunk" before you start.

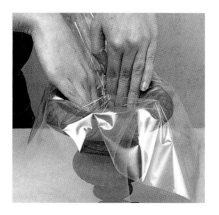

1 *Use a waterproof liner – such as cellophane – and push it into the shape of the container, with a little hanging over the edge.*

2 *Soak the foam; then cut off a piece with a knife to fit approximately the shape of the container. Shave off the corners and place in the container, pressing down for a tight fit and leaving about two inches above the top of the container. Now trim the liner and shave the foam to form the shape of the topiary.*

3 *Cover the rim with moss so the foam is well wedged in and the liner is hidden.*

Insert leaves at least half an inch into the foam so they can drink and make them into a fringe for the base of the topiary.

4 *Cut the flower heads allowing at least a 2-inch gap between the stem and the head. Cut at an oblique angle to expose the greatest area of the stem to the water.*

Starting at the base, insert the roses and complete the bottom layer by working upward row by row.

TECHNIQUES:

Wreaths

Wreaths can be as complex or as simple as you wish, and the choice of possible combinations of elements is endless. You can go simply for fresh flowers. You can use dried elements for a long-lasting wreath. You can mix interesting foliage with decorations such as cones or cinnamon sticks, dried orange, shells, or nuts. The underlying principle is the same for garlands. Always start with a firm base. Wreaths and garlands must have this strong underlying structure to support the weight of the flowers when they are added.

Always go in the same direction and secure each new piece of foliage or flower neatly with wire. A garland for a mantelpiece can be embellished after hanging. Put on the pieces that you want as features when you have already secured it firmly in place, so you'll be sure they're not hidden underneath.

1 *Make a wreath shape out of a strip of chicken wire, intertwining the ends to secure them.*

2 *Cover the chicken wire with moss, packing it in securely. Tie in the moss with wire as you go. Here, I've used raffia for a natural and pretty effect. Tie off the ends.*

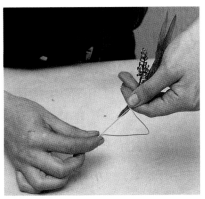

3 *Make little sprigs of flowers and foliage, tying them into little bunches. Take a piece of wire and bend it into a hairpin shape. Squeeze it so the arms of the hairpin are close together, and bend the wire to wrap one arm tightly around the stems two or three times.*

4 *The remaining straight arm is used to secure the sprig to the wreath. Simply plunge it into the moss, bending it back on the underside of the wreath. "Plant" each sprig so it covers the wire of the last one. When you have finished, the wires can be twisted together behind the wreath.*

Glossary of flower and plant names

FAMILY	US/IN BOOK	LATIN	UK
AGAVACEAE	Cordyline Dracaena	*Cordyline* *Dracaena*	Cordyline Dracaena
ALLIACEAE	Agapanthus Alliums	*Agapanthus* *Allium*	Agapanthus Alliums
AMARANTHACEAE	Celosia	*Celosia*	Celosia
AMARYLLIDACEAE	Amaryllis Daffodils Narcissus Nerines Paperwhites	*Hippeastrum* *Narcissus* *Narcissus* *Nerine* *Narcissus*	Amaryllis Daffodils Narcissus Nerines Jonquils
APIACEAE	Eryngiums	*Eryngium*	Eryngiums
ARACEAE	Arum lilies Calla lilies	*Zantedeschia* *aethiopica* *Calla palustris*	Arum lilies Bog arum
ARALIACEAE	Ivy	*Hedera*	Ivy
ARECACEAE	Kentia palm	*Howea*	Howea/Kentia
ASCLEPIADACEAE	Butterflyweed	*Asclepias*	Asclepias
ASPHODELACEAE	Eremurus	*Eremurus*	Eremurus
ASTERACEAE	Calendulas Carthamus Chrysanthemums Gerberas Marguerite daisies Rudbeckia Sunflowers	*Calendula* *Carthamus* *Chrysanthemum* *Gerbera* *Argyranthemum* *frutescens* *Rudbeckia* *Helianthus*	Marigold Carthamus Chrysanthemums Gerberas Marguerites Rudbeckia Sunflowers
BETULACEAE	Birch	*Betula*	Birch
BRASSICACEAE	Cabbages	*Brassica*	Cabbages
BROMELIACEAE	Guzmania Pineapple	*Guzmania* *Ananas*	Guzmania Pineapple
CAPRIFOLIACEAE	European cranberrybush Laurustinus	*Viburnum opulus* *Viburnum tinus*	Guelder rose Laurustinus
CARYOPHYLLACEAE	Carnations	*Dianthus*	Carnations
CLUSIACEAE	Hypericum	*Hypericum*	Hypericum
COLCHICACEAE	Gloriosa lilies	*Gloriosa*	Gloriosa lilies
CORNACEAE	Dogwood	*Cornus*	Dogwood
CUCURBITACEAE	Gourds Pumpkins	*Cucurbita* *Cucurbita*	Gourds Pumpkins
ERICACEAE	Rhododendron Salal	*Rhododendron* *Gaultheria shallon*	Rhododendron Shallon
EUPHORBIACEAE	Euphorbia Poinsettia	*Euphorbia* *Euphorbia* *pulcherrima*	Euphorbia/Spurge Poinsettia
FAGACEAE	Beech	*Fagus*	Beech
GENTIANACEAE	Lisianthus	*Lisianthus*	Lisianthus/Funeral flower

FAMILY	US/IN BOOK	LATIN	UK
HYACINTHACEAE	Hyacinths	*Hyacinthus*	Hyacinths
IRIDACEAE	Freesia Iris Montbretia	*Freesia* *Iris* *Crocosmia*	Freesia Iris Montbretia/ Crocosmia
LILIACEAE	Lilies Tulips	*Lilium* *Tulipa*	Lilies Tulips
LORANTHACEAE	Mistletoe	*Viscum album*	Mistletoe
MALVACEAE	Cottonbolls	*Gossypium* *hirsutum*	Cottonballs
MORACEAE	Ficus	*Ficus*	Figs
MUSACEAE	Bird of paradise Heliconias	*Strelitzia* *Heliconia*	Bird of paradise Heliconias
MYRTACEAE	Eucalyptus	*Eucalyptus*	Eucalyptus
OLEACEAE	Forsythia Jasmine Lilac	*Forsythia* *Jasminum* *Syringa*	Forsythia Jasmine Lilac
ORCHIDACEAE	Cymbidium orchids Singapore orchids	*Cymbidium* *Vanda* 'Miss Joaquim'	Cymbidiums Singapore orchids
PAPAVERACEAE	Iceland poppies Poppies	*Papaver nudicaule* *Papaver*	Iceland poppies Poppies
PINACEAE	Pine	*Pinus*	Pine
PITTOSPORACEAE	Pittosporum	*Pittosporum*	Pittosporum
PROTEACEAE	Grevillea Leucadendrum	*Grevillea* *Leucadendrum*	Grevillea Leucadendrum
RANUNCULACEAE	Anemones Christmas rose Delphiniums Hellebores Ranunculus	*Anemone* *Helleborus niger* *Delphinium* *Helleborus* *Ranunculus*	Anemones Christmas rose Delphiniums Helleborus Ranunculus
ROSACEAE	Cherry Cotoneaster Pyracantha Roses	*Prunus* *Cotoneaster* *Pyracantha* *Rosa*	Cherry Cotoneaster Pyracantha/ Firethorn Roses
RUBIACEAE	Gardenia	*Gardenia*	Gardenia
RUSCACEAE	Butcher's broom	*Ruscus aculeatus*	Butcher's broom/ Ruscus
SALICACEAE	Willow	*Salix*	Willow
SCROPHULARIACEAE	Veronica	*Veronica*	Veronica
SOLANACEAE	Peppers	*Capsicum*	Peppers
THEACEAE	Camellia	*Camellia*	Camellia
TYPHACEAE	Cattails	*Typha*	Reed mace
ZINGIBERACEAE	Ginger	*Zingiber*	Ginger

INDEX

CREDITS

Quarto would like to thank the following for providing pictures used in this book: Garden Picture Library page 37 and H. Smith pages 13, 61, and 85. All other photographs are the copyright of Quarto Publishing plc.

The author would like to thank his grandmother, for instilling a love of flowers in him from an early age, and

Jon and Luise for their professionalism and skill. Also, thanks to Bart and Henri at Holland Bloemen Export for supplying such fabulous flowers, and Tim at Blazing Bees for his ideas. The author and Quarto would like to thank Tamara Tipi for her invaluable contribution. Her inventive and skilful interpretation of the author's designs were an inspiration.

Quarto would also like to thank Browns Restaurant, 22 Jermyn Street and The Zinc Bar for providing the locations for some of the photographs.
Flower suppliers:
Holland Bloemen Export,
Aalsmeer, The Netherlands
Container suppliers:
Blazing Bees,
London, Great Britain